BUSHEL
& PECK
BOOKS

Published by Bushel & Peck Books, a family-run publishing house in Fresno, California, that
believes in uplifting children with the highest standards of art, music, literature, and ideas.
Find beautiful books for gifted young minds at www.bushelandpeckbooks.com.

Text and script copyright © Josep Sucarrats, 2020
Illustrations copyright © Miranda Sofroniou, 2020

First published in Spain by Editorial Flamboyant S.L.
under the title *Mercats, un món per descobrir*
www.editorialflamboyant.com

Translated by Tony Pesqueira
Edited by Emma Vetter

Type set in Dreaming Outloud, Tomarik, and Pen and Ink

Bushel & Peck Books is dedicated to fighting illiteracy all over the world. For every book we sell,
we donate one to a child in need—book for book. To nominate a school or organization
to receive free books, please visit www.bushelandpeckbooks.com.

LCCN: 2022945928
ISBN: 9781638191308

First Edition

Printed in China

10 9 8 7 6 5 4 3 2 1

Markets

A WORLD TO DISCOVER

JOSEP SUCARRATS   MIRANDA SOFRONIOU,
ILLUSTRATOR

Foreword

by Ferran Adrià, internationally renowned chef

During the summer some years ago, while I was opening the elBulli restaurant next to the waters and sand of the Mediterranean, I decided to dedicate a part of the rest of the year to traveling the world. That's how I came to learn about numerous new cuisines and ingredients for the first time. On one occasion, I went to the Amazon accompanied by my good friend Alex, who has a restaurant in São Paulo, and two more chefs, José and José Mari.

Alex showed us many different spices as we walked among the booths at the Ver-o-Peso market in Belém, a city at the river's edge in the state of Pará. I will never forget that trip. It was then that I realized that, although I cook and eat every day, there is still a lot for me to learn about cooking and food.

I would love for you to be able to go to Ver-o-Peso at least once in your life. But if, for whatever reason, you can't, you almost certainly have a market close to home where they sell food and drink. For many years, I went to a workshop next to one of the most famous markets in the world: la Boqueria in Barcelona. I would go every day! I still visit it every once in a while, and I always discover something new. Many merchants know the fruits, vegetables, meats, or fish that they sell better than anyone else. From these products, they can showcase delicious recipes and unsuspected curiosities.

All of this is why I willingly wrote the preface to this book (which was written and illustrated with such care). I feel at home at the market! On the following pages, you will see for yourself that markets are among the most interesting places, so long as you open your eyes.

When we visit markets, our minds are filled with questions, but we also find many answers. As such, I encourage you to visit markets often. On each page of this book, you will discover one of the markets that feed the locals in their corner of the world. You can be sure that there is no such thing as an inhabited place where people neither cook nor eat.

Did you know that one of the first skills that humans developed was cooking? Recognizing that we need to eat; knowing when and how to make food; learning what we can combine and what we can't; discovering what preservation or baking techniques improve food—humans have dedicated themselves to this for thousands and thousands of years!

If you are curious, you will find that any place on the planet will welcome you. If you can, we would love for you to come to elBulli to tell us everything that you have learned while you ate, drank, and cooked thanks to the markets that feed humanity.

Historic Markets

Every culture throughout humanity has had an organized system for selling and buying. The market has been the center of many cities since ancient times. It has served as a place for citizens to find what they need to live, and it has offered a space to meet up and exchange ideas and knowledge.

It is said that the first merchants in history were street vendors; in other words, the merchants went from place to place, loaded up with their goods to sell. Later on, they would get together on a set day and hour in a crowded area. Thus, the market was born!

GREEK AGORA

Plato, a philosopher from ancient Greece, explains that thanks to the markets and the people that would meet there, communities that ultimately became cities began to develop. In fact, the heart of Greek cities was the agora, a plaza where deals were closed, political speeches were heard, ideas were debated, and things were bought!

THE NATIVE AMERICAN CANOES

The Native American villages of North America exchanged different goods, often going up the rivers with their canoes full of raw materials and manufactured products. Since these were nomad villages, they would meet up at strategic places, where they would organize festivals. For example, Cahokia (in what is now the state of Illinois) was an important meeting place during the 11th and 12th centuries. It not only revitalized commerce throughout the whole area all along the Mississippi River, but it also revitalized the land politically, economically, and religiously.

THE ROMAN MACELLUM

If Greek cities had the agora, the Roman counterpart was the forum. However, as time passed, the Roman rulers preferred grouping food and commerce under the same roof. They built some buildings known as "macella," where all types of meat, fish, spices, and imported products from the known world were sold.

The Macellum in Rome was very important, and we know that it already existed in the 2nd century BC. Macella were rectangular, featuring rows of porticos with their market booths and even a pool in the center. They were decorated luxuriously because the rulers wanted to show off the city's power.

CARAVANS EN ROUTE TO KASHGAR

About 700 years ago, Marco Polo wrote: "Countless goods and merchandise arrive in Kashgar. The people live off of the shops and commerce. Many merchants that go around the world selling come out of this region." Thanks to Italian travelers, we know that the Kashgar Market in China was already important in the Middle Ages and, surely, long before. Even today, the market still fills up with sellers and buyers. Some travel over 1,000 miles to go there! All kinds of things are sold there: fabrics, shoes, clothes, crafts, livestock, etc. And in their taverns, they serve very hot bowls of noodles and meat when it's cold!

THE MEDIEVAL BEFFROI MARKET

During the Middle Ages in Europe, markets were the center of cities. They tended to be open-air markets situated close to churches, but the richest cities started to erect structures to organize them better and combine various services. Between the 12th and 15th centuries, people built the Beffroi Market in the Belgian city of Brussels. On the ground floor were butchers, spice sellers, and drapers (who sold bands, thread, yarn, buttons, etc.), and on the upper level you could find city hall.

THE AZTEC TIANGUIS

The Aztec civilization markets were called "tianguis" and could be found in lots of the Empire's communities. The most important one of all was in Tlatelolco, a city founded by the Aztecs in 1338 in what is now Mexico. In the city's center, they erected a temple, and in front of it was an enormous plaza with a tianguis. When the Spanish arrived, they were left in awe of this market—so much so that when they invaded the city, they almost didn't even touch it. Fruits and vegetables from the whole Aztec Empire were commercialized, but the novelty that fascinated them the most was cacao.

THE PATHS OF THE AUSTRALIAN ABORIGINES

During the time that Europe and Asia traded through the Silk Road, the Australian aborigines traded through sacred routes or paths that, according to their beliefs, their ancestors had blazed and remembered the way to through songs. The crossings of these paths (which were normally close to rivers or lagoons) were trading points. The aborigines understood commerce as a broad thing. Along with objects and products, they also exchanged songs, dances, stories, and rituals at their markets.

ISTANBUL'S GRAND BAZAAR

This market is often considered the oldest covered market that one can still visit. The sultans built it not long after conquering Istanbul more than five centuries ago. This was their way of showing their power to the residents. At first, it was a market that was dedicated to luxury products and objects. Each street was occupied by different craftsmen (jewelers, silk weavers, mat manufacturers, etc.) and the smell of tea, coffee, and spices. Overall, the Grand Bazaar has 58 streets and 4,000 shops!

What You Can Do at the Market

ONE GOES TO MARKETS TO BUY THINGS, BUT THEY ARE ALSO PLACES TO TRADE, BE ENTERTAINED, AND LEARN.

FILL THE PANTRY

HELP SUSTAINABILITY

ENJOY YOURSELF

LEARN TO COOK

EAT AND DRINK

MEET UP

FILL THE PANTRY

At the market, one can buy products that are fresh, having been cultivated, farmed, or fished from nearby. That way, the food has traveled less, and the flavor and nutritional properties are better preserved. Prepared products are also sold (such as bread, spices, drinks, sausages, etc.), as well as food from around the world.

HELP SUSTAINABILITY

Markets help the planet's sustainability because they offer products that are in proximity; thus, less packaging and plastic bags are used. In the same way, the Queen Victoria Market in Melbourne incentivizes domestic worm farms to reduce waste and produce fertilizer.

ENJOY YOURSELF

Markets are a spectacle: people left and right, colors, smells... it has been this way since the Middle Ages. Alongside merchants, there were musicians, acrobats, and dancers. The Jemaa el-Fnaa market of Marrakesh in Morocco still maintains this spirit. There are street artists on every corner. The Chatuchak Weekend Market of Bangkok in Thailand won't be boring either: when it opens, more than 200,000 people turn up!

In Baltimore, we find the oldest market in the United States, the Lexington Market. It is more than 200 years old! When the traditional horse race known as the Preakness Stakes is celebrated, the market organizes another race with crabs, their star product!

LEARN TO COOK

The shopkeepers are a well of culinary science! Listen closely to hear their tricks and advice. On top of that, many markets have opened cooking classes; some even schedule cooking workshops for children.

EAT AND DRINK

Many markets have at least one bar, and there are others that don't even have market booths—they rely on nearby restaurants and bars. One of the most beautiful ones is the San Miguel Market in Madrid.

Do you know what the French markets do? There are booths where you can take fish, meat, or vegetables that you just bought, and they prepare you a finger-licking-good plate.

MEET UP

Since their beginnings, markets were a place to meet up and get together with people from diverse backgrounds. If you go, for example, to the Cleveland West Side Market in the United States, you will see Polish, German, Irish, and Persian food booths; after all, the city was founded by and has grown with people arriving from all over the world.

People like to go to markets to correspond with others. They often start talking about recipes and cooking tricks, or they can end up talking about their whole life!

Markets have inspired works of art, movies, political ideas, and even revolutions. It is part of their charm.

What Is There at the Market?

Do you know why eating at markets helps us to vary our eating? Because you can find anything! At the best world markets, there are vegetables, fruit, meat, fish, and some foods that, despite being from the other side of the planet, make us feel at home. That being said, it's clear that the products can vary according to the country we are in. Do you recognize all of the ingredients that appear on these pages?

FRUIT

We like fruit because it is sweet, and a lot of fruits can quench our thirst. Eating fruit is a very healthy way to get more energy!

In countries with fewer hours of sunlight, fruit is less eye-catching, but as we get closer to the equator—the part of the planet that the sun touches the most—they gain color.

The city of Belém, in the state of Pará, Brazil, is the gateway to the Amazon forest. Its market, Ver-o-Peso, has more than 100 different types of fruit! The most popular is the azaí.

VEGETABLES

At a market, what would you say looks most like a jewelry store? The vegetable booths! Look— purple eggplants, red peppers, green zucchini, orange carrots... There are more colors during the summer, whereas in the winter—when the vegetables that grow underground are collected, like potatoes, sweet potatoes, or beets—the colors are dimmer.

GREENS

Little else provides us with so many vitamins and so much fiber.

The produce areas color the markets green, especially in the winter, when there are more vegetables. It is important to vary your vegetable purchases and know their properties well in order to follow a balanced diet. This is especially important now that there are more and more people who don't eat meat or fish. There are also vegetables under the water: seaweed! In countries like Japan, they use seaweed in many recipes. It is very healthy!

You would be surprised to see how many animals can appear on a menu.

MEATS

Meat is one of the most delicate foods. That's why, at the market, many customers look for a trusted butcher shop.

At poultry shops, they sell chicken and duck. In countries with big grasslands, like Argentina, they sell lots of beef, whether it be ox, cow, or veal. There is also often lamb. In the United States, China, and Europe, a lot of pork is consumed, but pork is usually avoided in Arab countries because Muslims don't eat pork.

FISH

What luck to be able to buy fish that just arrived at the harbor in the seaside town markets! For centuries, only the people who lived close to the ocean, rivers, or lakes ate fish. Today, thanks to refrigerated transport systems, they can arrive almost everywhere. If you go through the Saint John City Market in Canada, you will see the old ice room where they would preserve the fish before refrigerator rooms were invented. The biggest fish market in the world is in Tsukiji, Tokyo. At that market, 3,000 tons of 450 different species of fish arrive every day!

OTHER ANIMALS

Reptiles, insects, amphibians, crustaceans, bivalves... we humans eat everything. What would give you chills in some cultures is completely normal in others. Some edible species, like wild alligators, are at risk of extinction. However, some food sources are plentiful. Insects could feed lots of people in the future because they provide protein and are easy to breed. In Asia and in Latin America, people have been eating insects for centuries. To rediscover food, you need to experiment, mix, and combine flavors. Do you dare?

SPICES AND CONDIMENTS

You've surely tried pepper. It's possible that you have also tried saffron and cinnamon. Do cumin and chili ring a bell? Mustard? You could make a list of at least 150 ingredients that are classified as spices and condiments. They are used to give a different zing to meals. Certain spices are deeply rooted in some cultures, and these spices are usually at their respective culture's markets in abundance.

At the Központi Vásárcsarnok booths in Budapest, there tend to be strings of red chili peppers hanging. They call chili "paprika" there, and they add it to lots of recipes. It's almost a city symbol!

LEGUMES, GRAINS, AND SEEDS

Legumes provide lots of protein. If you play sports, they are essential! At the market, you can buy them raw, in grains, or baked. Some legumes and grains can be planted. A chickpea can grow into a chickpea plant, for example. But we also eat other types of seeds that aren't legumes, like pumpkin seeds, sunflower seeds, or chia seeds. They provide a lot of energy!

PRESERVES

Preserving food lets us eat it out of season or send it far away (since transporting it fresh would spoil it).

The oldest way to preserve food is draining the product (like dry tomatoes in Italy) or salting it (like cod from the Atlantic). Other foods that are preserved are meat and raw sausages (dried while hanging in rooms where the air takes away their water), jams (fruit or boiled vegetable compotes with sugar canned inside of airtight jars), or smoked food, among others.

THIS IS ALSO EATEN

If we are hungry, we will find some food to put in our mouths in almost every corner of the planet—at the market, of course. When you first travel and go into a market, you might think that everything is more or less like what you already know. But, especially if you travel far away, you will find food that will seem very strange—to you, of course! Because for the customers of those markets, it is quite normal. Now we'll go through the markets from around the world and fill our basket. Ready to be amazed? Be bold and be curious!

Durian. At the fruit stands from the Can Tho markets in Vietnam, they have a fruit with a rind that is filled with spikes called "durian." When it's opened, it reeks of dirty socks! For the Vietnamese, this is no problem. They are already used to the smell, and they tend to enjoy eating it. It is very nutritious.

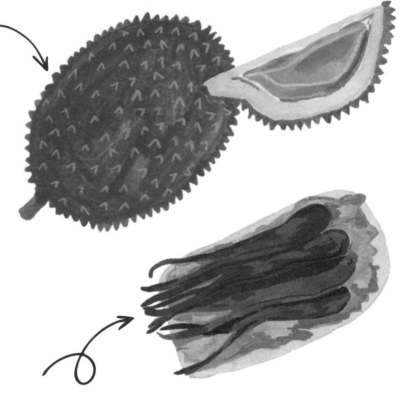

Spider. At the markets in the city of Skuon, Cambodia, they will offer you fried spiders. It is said that Cambodians have been eating them for more than 100 years. In the past, they were hungry and didn't have anything else. But now, spiders are a meal with some style! They fry them with garlic oil, and the spiders end up crunchy on the outside and soft on the inside.

Lizards. There are cultures for whom eating reptiles is not strange at all. In many places in Africa, they eat reptiles. At the biggest market on the continent, the Kejetia Market in the city of Kumasi, Ghana, they sell lizards.

Duck tongue. The day you visit Pekin, take a walk on the famous commercial street of Qianmen. There, you'll find the meat market. If you see some stretched-out strips of meat that you don't recognize...they are probably duck tongues! In China, they are considered a delicacy. They are eaten fried and baked, strung on skewers.

Grasshoppers. If you go to the Abastos Market in Oaxaca one day, it won't take you long to find the booths where they sell grasshoppers. These grasshoppers have been used in that part of the world for thousands of years. People eat them toasted, flavored with a little bit of lemon, salt, and garlic. For Mexicans, they are like sweets!

Barnacles. The barnacle is a very old animal; it hasn't changed for practically 30 million years. These crustaceans are incredibly difficult to eat. They don't have a head or eyes or anything; they look like a small piece of a branch. Picking them up on the rocks of the Galician coast in Spain is very dangerous because they are mostly found where the waves break strongly against the rocks. The percebeiros, the people who pluck and pick them, are exceptionally brave.

Snails. In prehistoric times, humans ate snails. Today, in countries like France, Spain, and Italy, they still like snails a lot. Before cooking them, they keep them in escargotières so that they can purge. This means, more or less, that they need to poop so that they can be completely clean! If eating them disgusts you, keep in mind that creams and cosmetics are made from the slime of some snails.

Puffer fish. In the Japanese city of Shimonoseki, there is an enormous fish market, the Karato Market. There, they sell the most expensive and the most dangerous fish in the world: the puffer fish (or, in Japanese, fugu). It is so toxic that it can cause death! In restaurants, only cooks that have taken a course on how to cook it can offer it. To the Japanese, it is such a delectable delicacy that the threat doesn't scare them, and they are willing to pay a lot of money to eat it.

Caviar. At the Danilovsky Market in Moscow, products arrive from all over the country and from neighboring republics. Along with fruits and vegetables, there are products like smoked fish, fresh cheese, or caviar that consists of roe from the sturgeon, a highly valued fish in Russia. The female sturgeon takes seven years to be fertile and give eggs. For that reason, caviar is very expensive.

Hákarl. In Reykjavík, you can find the Kolaportið Market next to the harbor. Enormous brown fish hang from the ceiling. They are hákarl, Greenland sharks that have been matured and dried. Preparing it takes a lot of work! When the fishermen arrive at the harbor with the shark, it is buried in a hole that is covered by rocks for two months. After that, it is hung to dry. If you aren't accustomed to it, it will seem to give off a terrifying stench. However, in Iceland, it is a traditional product.

Alfalfa juice. It's not surprising that, at the Iñaquito Market of Quito in Ecuador, there are so many juice stands. It is suffocatingly hot there! You can find orange juice, papaya juice, pineapple juice, mango juice, peach juice, blackberry juice, a mix of tropical fruit juices called "comeibebe," and alfalfa juice!

CAVIAR

PERU

IRAN

ICELAND

PERU

PORTUGAL

Where Does Food Come From?

We like to go to markets because we find fresh products from farmers and nearby fishermen there.

It's been like that for centuries! However, thanks to technology and to modes of transport, you can find food from all five continents at the market. Humanity has always come up with something to preserve food: salting it, draining it, canning it, freezing it...in this way, food has been able to travel without spoiling. Today, we have markets that are like a small planet!

TURKEY

UNITED KINGDOM

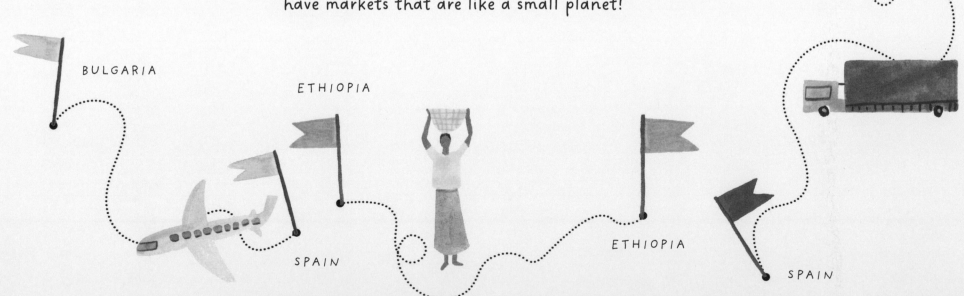

BULGARIA

ETHIOPIA

SPAIN

ETHIOPIA

SPAIN

CORN FROM THE SACRED INCA VALLEY, PERU

In Urubamba, in the Sacred Inca Valley, lots of corn is harvested. The field workers transport it to the impressive San Pedro de Cusco Central Market. Among the different varieties of corn that are cultivated in the country, there is a purple one that is used to prepare a drink called "chicha morada."

At this market, you will find endless ingredients that the Incas consumed, like chocolate, which takes up an entire hallway of the place. Other things are eaten that would surprise you, such as guinea pigs. It is a famous market because of the soups and the fruit juices, but many other products are prepared.

Corn is one of the most popular ingredients in the world.

SAN PEDRO DE CUSCO CENTRAL MARKET, PERU.
37 MILES BY DONKEY

21

PEPPERS FROM EL EJIDO, SPAIN

BOROUGH MARKET,
LONDON, UNITED KINGDOM.
1,400 MILES BY TRAILER

In El Ejido, Almería, there are miles and miles of greenhouses dedicated to the production of fruits and vegetables. Every day, hundreds of refrigerator trailers filled with red, green, and yellow peppers (as well as other products) leave the city to arrive at the great European markets. We know that just under 1,000 years ago, field workers were already going to sell their harvest at the place where the biggest market in London, the Borough Market, is currently found. Today, lots of food from Spain is sold there.

COD FROM ICELAND

The Portuguese are a fishing people—they are next to the Atlantic, after all! However, the fish that they consume the most is cod, and they go looking for it over 3,000 miles from their home, wandering in the icy waters of Iceland, Norway, or Russia. They discovered cod almost 1,000 years ago, and they learned to preserve it by salting and draining it. In this way, it was very easy to transport it by sea, and, since they fished a lot, they could

iRANiAN SAFFRON

Saffron and other spices were considered luxury items in the Middle Ages. Saffron is expensive, and it has an intense flavor—that's why such a small amount is used in cooking. On the Silk Road that joined China and Italy, saffron was used to trade. In 1663, in the Turkish city of Istanbul, they even built the Spice Bazaar. Today, there are still spice booths, but booths with other products like candy or dried fruit are more abundant.

Saffron arrives from Iran, the greatest global provider for this plant, via the highway from the city of Torbat-e Heydarieh, over 2,000 miles from Istanbul.

A kilo of saffron can come to be more expensive than a kilo of gold!

SPICE BAZAAR IN
ISTANBUL, TURKEY.
2,100 MILES BY TRUCK

9.00€   20.00

distribute cod throughout the country. The Bolhão Market in Oporto keeps the cod booths almost the same as they were 100 years ago.

Around the year 1000, the Basque fishermen specialized in cod fishing. Did you know that there is evidence that cod arrived in Terranova (Canada) centuries before Christopher Columbus touched down in America?

The Portuguese brag that they have more than 1,000 recipes for cooking cod!

BOLHÃO MARKET,
OPORTO, PORTUGAL.
3,100 MILES BY BOAT

LA BOQUERIA MARKET,
BARCELONA, SPAIN.
1,100 MILES BY PLANE

32€

24€ KILO

BULGARIAN MUSHROOMS

Wild mushrooms are a delicacy. In many countries, they are considered strange, while in others, it is common to eat them. For the Japanese and the French, for example, they are a basic cooking ingredient in the fall.

In Spain, especially in Catalunya, the same happens; when the mushroom season comes, there aren't enough mushrooms to cover the demand. That's why they are bought in other countries and regions where the same mushrooms—milk-cap, pumpkin mushrooms, hygrophores, etc.—are grown but aren't commonly eaten. In Bulgaria, there are forests in which these mushrooms are picked daily, and they arrive by plane to Barcelona after a few hours, very fresh.

MERCATO,
ADDIS ABABA,
ETHIOPIA.
6 MILES BY FOOT

ETHIOPIAN PAPAYAS

Africa's biggest market is in Addis Ababa, Ethiopia. It is known as the Mercato, and it has got you covered. You will find everything, from clothes to furniture to food. It is impossible to see it all in one day!

The fruit and vegetable area displays an incredible variety of products and colors. When the harvest is good, mangos, papayas, lemons, or oranges arrive from around the country. The field workers on the outskirts of Addis Ababa pick them and walk to the heart of the capital to sell them. Additionally, Ethiopia is famous for producing one of the best coffees in the world. At the Mercato, there are more than 100 booths where they sell it.

Not all markets are the same! Some are sheltered inside enormous boats covered by a roof while others are in the open air and rely on the sun. And, although almost all markets are put up at ground level, you can also find some that float on water.

There are markets for all tastes: crafts, books, artifacts, and ancient or second-hand objects...markets that are short-lived or thought to be for a particular occasion...and markets only for professionals.

Types of Markets

COVERED MARKETS

THESE ARE BEAUTIFUL, SPACIOUS, AND WELL-VENTILATED BUILDINGS, ALMOST ALWAYS BUILT WITH IRON-AND-GLASS STRUCTURES.

Two centuries ago, some English architects had the idea to cover the markets with a roof, because they were convinced that this would make markets more hygienic and comfortable. This is understandable given that, in England, it rains a ton! It is said that the first market that was covered was St Johns Shopping Centre in Liverpool in 1820. The covered markets idea was soon extended throughout the world. In 1872, for example, they inaugurated this practice in the Central Market of Santiago in Chile. It still exists and is considered one of the best in the world, especially because of the fish!

In Dakar, the capital of Senegal, there is the Marché Tilène. It is the city's most central market, and every day there is an uproar of vendors, buyers, cars, vehicles, animals, and so on. The field workers sell fruits and vegetables there, and sometimes they put their booths up outside the market.

ANY 3 FRUITS

BOROUGH CHEESE COMPANY

OPEN-AIR MARKETS

THESE ARE PLACED OUTSIDE, NORMALLY IN PLAZAS. THEY CAN BE PUT UP AND TAKEN DOWN DAILY, RUN FOR SEVERAL DAYS IN A ROW, OR OPEN ONLY ON CERTAIN DAYS OF THE WEEK.

Throughout a large part of Africa, it rains very little. It's unsurprising, then, that almost all of the markets there are open-air. One of the biggest and most boisterous markets is the one they put up every Monday at the esplanade in front of the Great Mosque of Djenné in Mali. Everything is sold, from clothes to animals to the most typical ingredients from the country's gastronomy: noodles, pumpkins, spices, etc. There are also booths where they cook. If you ever go and try the plates, you would be best off with a water bottle in hand; the plates are very spicy!

In Guatemala, we find the Chichicastenango Market. It is beautiful, full of color from the fruit and vegetables, the typical Guatemalan fabrics, and the flowers that are sold on the stairs of the Santo Tomás church.

FLOATING MARKETS

THESE MARKET BOOTHS ARE BOATS. THEY JOSTLE ON THE DOCKS OF LIFTED CITIES NEXT TO BIG RIVERS. DUE TO THE LACK OF SUITABLE SPACE ON LAND, THESE MARKETS HAVE SUCCEEDED IN WINNING OVER SPACE ON THE WATER.

Floating markets are very typical in Southeast Asia in countries like Myanmar, Thailand, and Vietnam. The world's most famous one is Damnoen Saduak in Thailand. The vendors are field workers and fishermen who live in towns next to the river. They go down to the city in boats filled with products...and they don't need to unload them! They offer the products from the boats themselves, and when they've sold it all, they row home.

Although it can seem difficult to know what each boat sells, these markets have an order to things. At the Cai Rang Market, in the Vietnamese city of Can Tho, booths that offer similar products are next to one another. Additionally, there are boats that hang samples of what they sell high on a vertical pole so that they can be seen from afar.

OTHER MARKETS

There are some types of markets so special that we give them a particular name. Of course, they are still markets, but if we refer to them by their specific names, we will easily know what type of market they are. Most of them sell food, but others don't. Despite their differences, if you go to them, you will see how the environment there—which is one that you can almost breathe—is very similar to other markets.

Encantes. Outside some markets in Barcelona, terraced to the front, are booths for clothing, house products, shoes, and other goods. These small markets aren't food markets. They are called "encantes." In Barcelona, there is also an enormous market known as the Mercat dels Encants dedicated to furniture and secondhand or older belongings. In many cities, we find this type of market, although they have different names. In Madrid, they are called "rastros." In Paris, Brussels, or Prague, they are given a very fun name: "flea markets."

Souks and bazaars. The markets in Islamic cities (that is to say, where the predominant religion is Islam) are called "souks" or "bazaars." The Khan el-Khalili Market in Cairo is important to note, but the markets in Marrakesh, Tunisia, or Istanbul are also worth mentioning. They tend to be situated at the heart of the city, and they bring together jewelry, mat, furniture, or cooking utensil booths. Most of them are open-air, but some are in beautiful medieval buildings.

One of the biggest ones is Iran's Grand Bazaar of Tehran. Despite being very famous for its jewelry and its watches, it also sells traditional food, especially dried fruit and raisins.

Quick note! If you go shopping there, you will need to haggle!

Auction markets. In the Middle Ages, auction markets in the Mediterranean were places where merchants closed out commercial deals. They were fundamental to the economy; in some cities, the beautiful buildings that were built to host them still exist.

Today, the biggest auction market in the world is in Toyosu, Japan. This auction is actually a fish market. At the important ports, it's all about the building where the fishermen take the fresh fish to put it up for auction. Each box of fish is presented to the buyers at an initial price. Then, those who are interested in buying it start to bid. Whoever offers the highest price takes home the

Whoever offers the highest price takes home the fish!

fish. The buyers are fishmongers or professional cooks; they are the only ones who can participate in the market auctions.

At the edge of the Indian Ocean is Dar es-Salaam, one of the most important cities in Tanzania. Many of its inhabitants meet each morning at the city's auction market to participate in the fish and seafood auction for fish recently brought in from the sea.

Wholesale markets. Wholesale markets are immense and look like cities in and of themselves. They have their own network of streets—dozens of buildings are needed to exhibit the whole market. To enter, you often have to pay a toll or ask for a special permit. This is because these are markets for professionals that purchase things in great quantities, such as vegetable preserve companies, cooks from big restaurants, heads of school cafeterias and hospital kitchens...or the vendors from the markets where you shop, of course!

The biggest wholesale food market in the world is the Marché International de Rungis in the Paris suburbs. Everything they sell is impressive. You can even find hundreds of types of cheese!

How We Pay

You already know it: at the shops, everything has a price! There are lots of people who earn a living selling goods. That's why, since prehistoric times, humans have invented systems to pay for the products or services that we need. Depending on what market you go to, you will need to pay in one way or another. And you can find totally different customs in different places.

BARTERING

Just imagine: bartering is an ancient method that was invented in Neolithic times, more than 5,000 years ago! At that time, they realized that one person could not manage to do everything necessary for society to thrive. That's why they decided to exchange products and services. Thousands of years later, there are markets where things are still bought in this way. In Ethiopia, for example, the Konso craftsmen exchange their pieces at the market for meat or milk from the Bodi shepherds.

COINS AND BILLS

The Greeks invented the coin 2,700 years ago, upon finding that it was difficult to compensate everyone fairly when bartering.

If coins were used to buy and sell, the price for each thing could be clearly indicated.

Paper bills, however, have only existed for 300 years; they were used for the first time in Sweden.

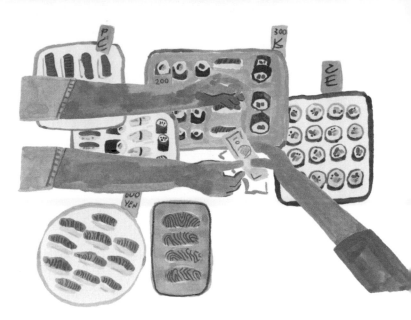

CARDS AND MOBILE PHONES

A lot of the time, people pay with a plastic card that is inserted in or brought close to a machine. We're talking about an electronic card created by an American bank 60 years ago. As you pay, the money for the purchase goes from your bank account to the vendor's.

Electronic payments have become so sophisticated that, today, a lot of people pay with their cell phone or even with their smartwatch.

BARGAINING

In some countries, the price of products is indicated by a tag or a sign, and it doesn't change. But in other places—especially in Arab and African countries and in some corners of South America—the buyer and the vendor have to bargain. In other words, they have to agree on the price of the goods. Starting at the marked price, the buyer proposes a reduction, the vendor asks for a little more money, the buyer proposes a discount once more...and that's how it continues until they arrive at a price that satisfies both.

Aparapita. The aparapita carries the purchases of the market's customers. They can be found, for example, at the Rodríguez de La Paz Market in Bolivia.

Greengrocer

Fishmonger

Butcher

Chef

Florist

Markets Are People

At the market, the people who sell and buy are as important—or even more so—than what is sold and bought.

Water carrier. At souks, there is a typical street vendor who is loaded with a big container full of water to give drinks to everyone who asks.

Shipper

Vendor

Health inspector. There are all kinds of inspectors. The health inspectors ensure that no unsafe or bad products are sold. Some are veterinarians, and they supervise the quality of the meat.

Craftsman

Spice seller

Tourist

Field worker

Cleaner

Vendor families. In many circumstances, several generations of the same family will work at the same booths. As such, they know a lot about what they are selling.

And the customers!

Markets That Appear in This Book

In this book, almost fifty markets are named from around the world. Even so, you surely have one close by that doesn't appear on the list. Are you up for discovering it?

JOSEP SUCARRATS

What this journalist likes most is good food and good conversation. If you can combine both of those activities, even better. That is why, since the twenty-first century began, he has dedicated himself to writing and talking about gastronomy. He is the director of the magazine *Cuina* and a regular contributor to radio, television, and digital media gastronomy spaces. He has cowritten a book about Barcelona cuisine and another about the vermouth phenomenon, and he has published a recipe book dedicated to macaroni. He would travel to any corner of the world to try a good meal, but he is also in love with the wine that his family makes from the grapes on the vines at the house where he was born.

MIRANDA SOFRONIOU

Miranda Sofroniou is a British illustrator who lives in Melbourne, Australia. She graduated in Illustration from the University of the Arts London (Camberwell College of Arts). Trips and nature inspire her, which she depicts in rich and colorful illustrations. She uses traditional painting techniques like water-based, watercolor, and acrylic, and she combines free brushstrokes with abundant detail. With the objective of evoking a determined atmosphere and awakening a feeling of exploration and surprise, she creates narrative worlds with the necessary enchantment to invite the public to enter them and enjoy her personal interpretation of the life that surrounds us.